Instant Yii 1.1 Application Development Starter

Get started with building attractive PHP web applications with the Yii framework

Jacob Mumm

Mark Safronov

BIRMINGHAM - MUMBAI

Instant Yii 1.1 Application Development Starter

First published: June 2013

Production Reference: 1300513

Published by Packt Publishing Ltd.
Livery Place
35 Livery Street
Birmingham B3 2PB, UK.

ISBN 978-1-78216-168-4

www.packtpub.com

Credits

Authors

Jacob Mumm

Mark Safronov

Reviewer

Sergey Malyshev

Acquisition Editors

Andrew Duckworth

Kunal Parikh

Commissioning Editor

Harsha Bharwani

Technical Editor

Varun Pius Rodrigues

Project Coordinator

Deenar Satam

Proofreader

Paul Hindle

Graphics

Abhinash Sahu

Production Coordinator

Prachali Bhiwandkar

Cover Work

Prachali Bhiwandkar

Cover Image

Conidon Miranda

About the Authors

Jacob Mumm is a web developer from Upstate New York specializing in PHP and JavaScript web applications. He has worked for non-profit organizations, advertising companies, and schools using tools such as Drupal, jQuery (including UI and Mobile), AngularJS, and the Yii Framework. His interests range from outdoor activities such as hiking, camping, and kayaking, to organic food and gardening as part of a holistic, sustainable lifestyle, all the while staying up to date with the latest gadgets, gizmos, and web application technologies.

One of the things he deeply enjoys is talking to people about the things for which he has the most passion. He likes to share his knowledge and experience with others. Even when incomplete, Jacob finds the act of consolidating his thoughts on a subject a great way to solidify his own understanding or to discover places where he needs to investigate further.

This book is dedicated to Joseph Fitzsimmons, because he has heard me explain quite a lot of things in recent years. Joe is a good friend who I have had the pleasure of watching and helping grow from someone fiddling with HTML to a degree-holding, up-and-coming web programmer. Joe embodies the target audience for this book, as he has the basis for technical understanding and is ready to take the next step into framework-driven development. This book was written largely by me pretending to be explaining things to Joe.

Mark Safronov is a professional web application developer from the Russian Federation with experience and interest in a wide range of programming languages and technologies. He has built and participated in building different types of web applications, from purely computational ones to full-blown e-commerce sites. He is also a proponent of following the current best practices for test-first development and clean and maintainable code.

He is currently employed at Clevertech, and is working on Yii-based PHP web applications and maintaining a quite popular YiiBooster open source extension.

Back in 2008, he translated the book *Visual Prolog 7.1 for Tyros* by Eduardo Costa in to Russian.

About the Reviewer

Sergey Malyshev is an IT specialist from Ukraine. He has been working in the IT industry for more than 15 years, 8 years of which he has devoted to the development of web applications. Out of conviction that it's impossible to become a great specialist in all areas at the same time, he has chosen for himself PHP, MySQL, and JavaScript as top priority directions. During his career, Sergey took part in developing dozens of different websites, social networks, CMS, CRM, and ERP systems. He was not only a developer, but also an architect, a project manager, and a technical consultant. Apart from participating in the realization of some technical projects, he also organized various advanced training courses for IT specialists in the companies where he was employed. As he has a degree in management, Sergey took part in the business process automation of companies specializing in software development.

At present, Sergey holds the position of a software engineer in the company SugarCRM and deals with the development of one of the most popular customer relationship management systems in the world. Before that, he worked on the development of applications based on Yii Framework. These include the search engine for real estate company `livingthere.com` and the corporate CMS system WebModulite for New York design agency Blue Fountain Media. Participation in these projects and also work on his own extension for debugging Yii applications, YiiDebugToolbar, has helped Sergey get vast experience and expert knowledge of Yii Framework.

www.packtpub.com

Support files, eBooks, discount offers and more

You might want to visit www.PacktPub.com for support files and downloads related to your book.

Did you know that Packt offers eBook versions of every book published, with PDF and ePub files available? You can upgrade to the eBook version at www.PacktPub.com and as a print book customer, you are entitled to a discount on the eBook copy. Get in touch with us at service@ packtpub.com for more details.

At www.PacktPub.com, you can also read a collection of free technical articles, sign up for a range of free newsletters and receive exclusive discounts and offers on Packt books and eBooks.

packtlib.packtpub.com

Do you need instant solutions to your IT questions? PacktLib is Packt's online digital book library. Here, you can access, read and search across Packt's entire library of books.

Why Subscribe?

- ✦ Fully searchable across every book published by Packt
- ✦ Copy and paste, print and bookmark content
- ✦ On demand and accessible via web browser

Free Access for Packt account holders

If you have an account with Packt at www.PacktPub.com, you can use this to access PacktLib today and view nine entirely free books. Simply use your login credentials for immediate access.

Table of Contents

Instant Yii 1.1 Application Development Starter

Welcome to *Instant Yii 1.1 Application Development Starter*. This book has been designed as a crash course in web application development with the Yii Framework. You will learn a step-by-step approach to building database-driven websites utilizing the features and extensions available in Yii.

This book contains the following sections:

So, what is Yii? – In this section, we'll start with a short review of what the Yii framework is, how it got started, and the overall benefits you'll get when you start using it.

Installation – In this section, we'll install Yii Framework and kickstart your first "Hello World" application with it.

Quick start – Given the automatically-generated example application, we extend it to be a rudimentary blog according to the blog example from the Yii website, while also learning a lot of the most important concepts in Yii along the way.

Top 5 features you need to know about – In this section, we continue the practical examples and we explore some not so obvious details and tricks of the framework, which can really help you in developing your application.

People and places – Lastly, we'll see where to seek help and how to get to know the quite vast Yii community.

So, what is Yii?

Yii is an open source framework for web applications built with the PHP scripting language. It was first released late in 2008 to a world bustling with frameworks vying for market share. Although it entered the game somewhat late, this turned out to be an advantage as its creator, Qiang Xue, was able to include some of the best features of existing products in Yii. Also, the lessons he learned as a developer for the Prado framework helped him to build a superior solution. Today, Yii is widely heralded as one of the top PHP web frameworks. You can read more about it at `http://www.yiiframework.com`.

As opposed to the **Content Management Systems** (**CMS**), it is not a complete skeleton of your website, which is configurable by some sort of graphical user interface. You have probably heard the names Joomla! and Drupal, which are particularly famous CMS examples in the PHP world.

On the contrary, Yii is called a framework because it has a set of built-in components. You, as a web application developer, can and definitely should freely use these to save your development time.

So, whether you just need a quick database app, some web services, or you have been tasked with building a whole corporate web portal, Yii will lay the groundwork and set you on the right path.

Probably the most important parts of Yii are the complete database access layer and the highly intricate page rendering system. It comes with pre-built smart UI controls like the data grids or something simpler like datepickers, ready to be used on web pages. Also, for many routine coding tasks there are a set of automatic code generators. All of this will be explained in further sections.

The Yii website also contains a huge number of user-contributed extensions to help you add functionality quickly. Applications built with the Yii clean organization style turn out highly extensible and easy to maintain.

Yii enforces a tried and true architecture for your application, known as **Model View Controller** (**MVC**). This structure utilizes object-oriented principles to make clean separations in code organization.

Controllers receive requests, instantiate and manipulate the models that do the real work, and finally render the views for interaction with the end user. This will be discussed in later sections to a greater depth; however, it'll be important to know that unlike in the original MVC definition, views in Yii are completely passive, being just the page templates and not the full-fledged classes.

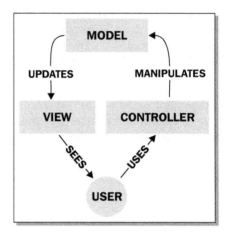

Yii's speed is unmatched thanks to some intelligent design choices at the core level. Most frameworks lose performance when they load more functionality than required for a given request. Loading too many classes can mean more disk reads, as each class is generally stored in its own file, or at least more processing if scripts are cached. More classes generally also result in additional database transactions, and all of these operations are both time and resource consuming.

Yii sticks to a philosophy of lazy-loading, where it strives not to load classes until they are actually needed. The core framework also adds no additional tables to your database, and makes only the minimum number of requests required to fetch the data for a given action. When your app is ready for production, there are a number of caching options to take performance to the next level. To reduce file I/O, Yii has built-in components that encapsulate common data caching solutions such as APC, Memcached, XCache, and EAccelerator. It also has a few components to handle caching of computed application data for an appropriate amount of time, such as the result of a complex database query.

Nowadays, when a website allows users to post content, it runs the risk that some of that content might actually be malicious code. Probably the most frequent are **SQL Injection, Cross-Site Scripting (XSS)**, and **Cross-site Request Forgery (CSRF)** attacks. Of course, you can look up these terms in Wikipedia, but you can also look up the detailed review of all these types of attacks in the *Web Application Hacker's Handbook*, by Stuttard Pinto, printed by Wiley in 2011. These are the common problems that website developers must address when accepting form data. Yii has built-in means to cope with them. All database interactions made properly by the Yii API sanitize user input automatically.

For dealing with user-generated content that will be rendered on the web pages, Yii encapsulates a project called **HTML Purifier,** which can be applied to any input field and will filter out any malicious code, unless specified on a white list. The homepage of the project is http://htmlpurifier.org/, and it is included in the component.

For automatic protection from CSRF attacks of all your forms altogether, there is a single switch-in configuration. It will pass a random value to a user when they load a form. By having this value passed back, the interaction is validated.

All these features will be explained later in the *Top features* section.

Downloading the example code

You can download the example code files for all Packt books you have purchased from your account at http://www.PacktPub.com. If you purchased this book elsewhere, you can visit http://www.PacktPub.com/support and register to have the files e-mailed directly to you.

Installation

Yii is a web application framework, so the first thing you need is a web server. Yii is capable of running on most common HTTP servers, but the platform of choice for project maintainers and testers is Apache on Linux. NGINX is also a good choice, and you can also run Yii on Windows servers with Apache or Microsoft's IIS server.

All instructions in this section assume the Linux (or Mac OS) environment with an Apache server.

Server requirements

As Yii is a PHP framework, the main dependency of Yii is PHP (version 5.1.0 or higher). Yii also makes use of a few key PHP extensions. These include PDO for MySQL or PostgreSQL, the DOM extension, Mcrypt for security, SOAP, and GD for image processing. For data caching, it requires either Memcache, APC, XCache, or EAccellerator, all of which are optional. Yii supports database solutions such as MySQL 4.1 or greater, PostgreSQL 7.3 and above, SQLite 2 and 3, Microsoft SQL Server 2000 or later, and Oracle. Depending on which database is selected for the project, the appropriate PHP extension will be required. Please note that you don't need a database at all to use Yii in your application, however, you'll definitely lose a lot of data persistence solutions built in the framework.

Step 1 – Setting up Yii

Let's start from the assumption that you already have the following things:

+ A running and configured web server such as Apache
+ A folder published as a webroot of a website accessible from your browser

So the only thing you need to set up right now is a real website in this webroot folder. Properly doing this two things is surely out of scope of this book.

The place where you get the Yii framework bundle is the downloads section at the official website (direct URL is `http://www.yiiframework.com/download`). For application development, you need a stable version packaged in the archive file. You don't need to get the sources of Yii from a GitHub or Subversion repository unless you want to fiddle with the framework itself.

The ideology behind Yii is that the framework itself lies outside of your application directory, preferably in some system directory with root user access only. The framework's folder should be configured so only your web server will have rights to read the files in it. This policy is to prevent the unwanted direct access to framework files by the request to web server. When you create your application, you also configure its real path to the Yii directory.

In short, for Linux systems with a web server running as the user apache, you can install Yii Version 1.1.13. e9e4a0 from the command line as follows:

```
# cd /var/local/
# wget http://yii.googlecode.com/files/yii-1.1.13.e9e4a0.tar.gz
# tar -zxf yii-1.1.13.e9e4a0.tar.gz && rm yii-1.1.13.e9e4a0.tar.gz
# chown -R apache yii-1.1.13.e9e4a0
```

 Note that for working in a system folder like /var/local, you need to be a root user. Of course, you can use any directory you like.

Inside the resulting yii directory, you'll find three folders named as follows:

+ demos
+ framework
+ requirements

The requirements folder is a helper to make a self test for your server setup. You can copy it to your webroot folder and access http://your.website.address/requirements/index.php from the web browser to see whether your system complies to the framework's requirements.

The framework folder is the Yii framework itself. You essentially only need its contents to use Yii in your application. From now on, we'll refer to the path under which Yii is installed as path-to-yii.

Step 2 – Creating your project

Once you have the framework installed on your machine, there is a command-line tool called yiic that is capable of building the skeleton application, among other quite numerous things. Open a console, navigate to your webroot, then run the autogenerator command:

```
$ path-to-yii/framework/yiic webapp sitename
```

The sitename token is the path to your new application. As you are already in your webroot folder, you just need to provide a name of a subfolder and not a full path to it.

This shell script is intended for use on Linux, so if you are on Windows, there is a yiic.bat file. Both scripts essentially run framework/yiic.php with the PHP command-line executable on your system, so the alternative method is to run it as follows:

```
$ php path-to-yii/framework/yiic.php webapp sitename
```

Before you can visit your site, you must check the index.php file to make sure it points to the actual Yii installation folder.

Make sure you have a line that looks like this in `sitename/index.php`:

```
$yii='path-to-yii/framework/yii.php';
```

You can now visit your site and see the basic hello world website with a homepage, about, contact, and a login page. As the application was created in a subfolder of your `webroot` folder, the URL should be like this: `http://your.website.address/sitename`.

And that's it!!

Your application folder will contain the following structure under the `sitename` folder:

+ `assets`: Contains published resource files
+ `css`: Contains CSS files
+ `images`: Contains image files
+ `themes`: Contains application themes
+ `protected`: Contains protected application files

The protected folder contains the following directories:

+ `commands`: Contains customized yiic commands
+ `components`: Contains reusable user components
+ `config`: Contains configuration files
+ `controllers`: Contains controller class files
+ `data`: Contains the sample database
+ `extensions`: Contains third-party extensions
+ `messages`: Contains translated messages
+ `models`: Contains model class files
+ `runtime`: Contains temporarily generated files
+ `tests`: Contains test scripts
+ `views`: Contains controller view and layout files

The `views` folder contains the following directories:

+ `layouts`: Contains layout view files
+ `site`: Contains view files for the site controller

Quick start – creating an application

The Yii website contains, among its wonderful documentation, a tutorial on how to build a basic blog application, which is one of the included demos in the framework source. It's in **Tutorials | The Yii Blog Tutorial** section. The direct URL is `http://www.yiiframework.com/doc/blog/`.

Let's use this example while we explain the aspects of Yii-based applications. We will not repeat the complete example here, of course, because you can read it in full on the website.

Step 1 – planning the workflow

When you write a real application, you should start with the requirements regarding application functionality. For the blog example, this is described in the Getting Started: Requirements Analysis section at the very beginning of the tutorial. The direct URL is `http://www.yiiframework.com/doc/blog/1.1/en/start.requirements`.

After you have written all the desired features, you basically start implementing them one by one. Of course, in serious software development there's a lot of gotchas included, but overall it's the same.

The blog example is a database driven application, so we need to prepare a database schema beforehand. Here's what they came up with for the blog demo:

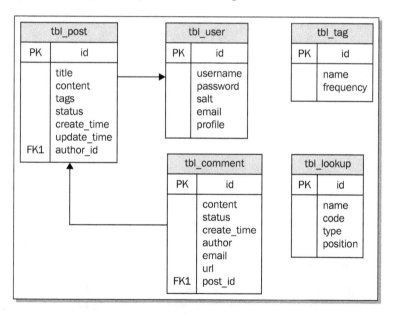

This image is a verbatim copy from the blog example demo. Note that there are two links missing. The posts table has a `tags` field, which is the storage area for tags written in raw and is not a foreign key to the `tags` table. Also, the `author` field in `comment` should really be the foreign key to the `user` table. Anyways, we'll not cover the actual database generation, but I suggest you do it yourself. The blog tutorial at the Yii website has all the relevant instructions addressed to total newbies.

Next in this section, we will see how easy it is with Yii to get a working user interface that will be able to manipulate our database.

Step 2 – linking to the database from your app

Once you design and physically create the database in some database management system like MySQL or maybe SQLite, you are ready to configure your app to point to this database. The skeleton app generated by the `./yiic webapp` command needs to be configured to point to this database. To do this, you need to set a `db` component in the main `config` file located at `protected/config/main.php`. There is a section that contains an array of components. Following is the setup for a MySQL database located at the same server as the web application itself. You will find a commented-out template for this already present when you generate your app:

/protected/config/main.php

```
'components'=>array(
    /* other components */
    'db'=>array(
        'connectionString' => 'mysql:host=localhost;dbname=DB_NAME,
        'emulatePrepare' => true,
        'username' => YOUR_USERNAME,
        'password' => YOUR_PASSWORD,
        'charset' => 'utf8',
    ),
    /* other components */
),
```

This is a default component having a `CDbConnection` class and is used by all of our ActiveRecord objects which we will create later. As with all application components, all configuration parameters correspond to the public properties of the component's class; so, you can check the API documentation for details.

By the way, you really need to understand more about the main application config. Read about it in the *Definitive Guide to Yii* on the official website at **Fundamentals | Application | Application Configuration**. The direct URL is `http://www.yiiframework.com/doc/guide/1.1/en/basics.application#application-configuration`.

Just remember that all configuration parameters are just properties of the CWebApplication object, which you can read about in the API documentation; the direct URL is http://www.yiiframework.com/doc/api/1.1/CWebApplication.

Step 3 – generating code automatically

Now that we have our app linked up to a fully built database, we can start using one of Yii's greatest features: automatic code generation. To get started, there are two types of code generation that are necessary:

✦ Generate a model class based on the tables in your database

✦ Run the CRUD generator that takes a model and sets up a corresponding controller and a set of views for basic listing, creating, viewing, updating, and deleting from the table

The console way

There are two ways to go about automatic code generating. Originally, there was only the yiic tool used earlier to create the skeleton app. For the automatic code generation features, you would use the yiic shell index.php command, which would bring up a command-line interface where you could run subcommands for modeling and scaffolding.

```
$ /usr/local/yii/framework/yiic shell index.php
Yii Interactive Tool v1.1 (based on Yiiv1.1.13)
Please type 'help' for help. Type 'exit' to quit.
>> model Post tbl_post
   generate models/Post.php
   unchanged fixtures/tbl_post.php
   generate unit/PostTest.php
The following model classes are successfully generated:
    Post
If you have a 'db' database connection, you can test these models now
with:
    $model=Post::model()->find();
    print_r($model);


>> crud Post
   generate PostController.php
   generate PostTest.php
mkdir /var/www/app/protected/views/post
```

```
generate create.php

generate update.php

generate index.php

generate view.php
```

As you can see, this is a quick and easy way to perform the `model` and `crud` actions. The `model` command produces just two files:

✦   For your actual model class

✦   For unit tests

The `crud` command creates your controller and view files.

Gii

Console tools may be the preferred option for some, but for developers who like to use graphical tools, there is now a solution for this, called **Gii**.

To use Gii, it is necessary to turn it on in the main `config` file: `protected/config/main.php`. You will find the template for it already present, but it is commented out by default. Simply uncomment it, set your password, and decide from what hosts it may be accessed. The configuration looks like this:

```
'gii'=>array(
    'class'=>'system.gii.GiiModule',
    'password'=>'giiPassword',

    // If removed, Gii defaults to localhost only.
    // Edit carefully to taste.
    'ipFilters'=>array('127.0.0.1','::1'),

    // For development purposes,
    // a wildcard will allow access from anywhere.
    // 'ipFilters'=>array('*'),
),
```

Once Gii is configured, it can be accessed by navigating to the app URL with `?r=gii` after it, for example, `http://www.example.com/index.php?r=gii`. It will begin with a prompt asking for the password set in the `config` file. Once entered, it will display a list of generators. If the database is not set in the `config` file, you will see an error when you attempt to use one.

The most basic generator in Gii is the model generator. It asks for a table name from the database and a name to be used for the `PHP` class.

Note that we can specify a table name prefix, which will be ignored when generating the model class name. For instance, the blog demo's user table is `tbl_user`, where the `tbl_` is a prefix. This feature exists to support some setups, especially common in shared hosting environments, where a single database holds tables for several distinct applications. In such an environment, it's a common practice to prefix something to names of tables to avoid getting into naming conflict and to easily find tables relevant to some specific application. So, as these prefixes don't mean anything in the application itself, Gii offers a way to automatically ignore them. Model class names are being constructed from the remaining table names by the obvious rules:

✦ Underscores are converted to uppercasing the next letter

✦ The first letter of the class name is being uppercased as well

The first step in getting your application off the ground is to generate models for all the entity tables in your database. Things such as bridge tables will not need models, as they simply relate two entities to one another rather than actually being a distinct thing. Bridge tables are being used for generating relations between models, expressed in the `relations` method in model class.

For the blog demo, the basic models are User, Post, Comment, Tag, and Lookup.

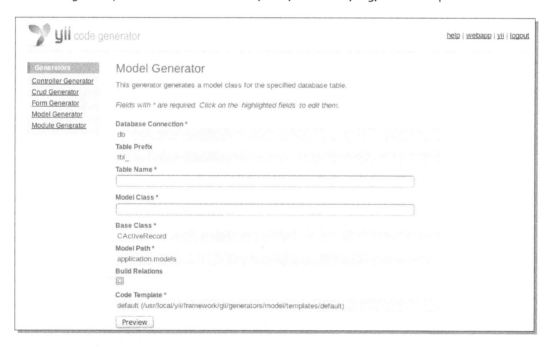

The second phase of scaffolding is to generate the CRUD code for each of these models. This will create a controller and a series of view templates. The controller (for example, `PostController`) will handle routing to actions related to the given model. The view files represent everything needed to list and view entities, as well as the forms needed to create and update individual entities.

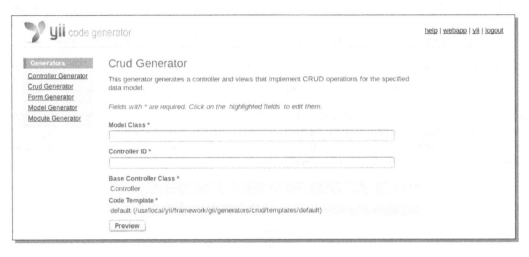

For all the generators, you will start with a form where you fill in either a **Table Name** field for the **Model Generator** page, or a **Model Class** field for the **Crud Generator** page. Afterward, you will have to hit the **Preview** button, which will show you exactly what files will be created. Finally, you must hit the **Generate** button for the actions to take place.

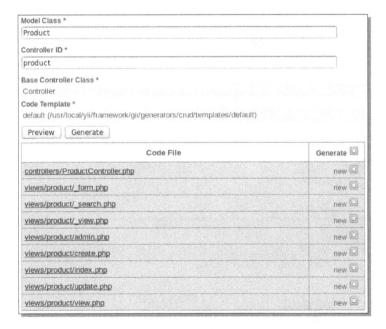

Step 4 – looking at the components of Yii

So now that you've seen the basics of what is being created here, let's take a deeper look at these components.

Models

Yii's models are just PHP classes that extend from the CModel base class. The framework already contains two helper subclasses of CModel: CFormModel and CActiveRecord.

While CFormModel is just a semantic wrapper around the concept of a user-submitted HTML form, CActiveRecord is a complete implementation of an ActiveRecord design pattern.

It is a well known and commonly used pattern for database driven applications. Yii got a lot of inspiration in this area from the Rails framework for Ruby, which has what is widely considered to be one of the best implementations of ActiveRecord. As with any other design pattern (even MVC), you can read about it in the definitive book *Design Patterns: Elements of Reusable Object-Oriented Software* by Ralph Johnson.

To make things simple, ActiveRecord is an object-oriented pattern that calls for a one-to-one mapping of database tables to classes (for example, tbl_post to Post model, tbl_comment to Comment model). In its original definition, ActiveRecord is not really a one-to-one mapping (one class can use any number of tables for storing data), but ActiveRecords in Yii work this way.

Instances of a model class will have properties that correspond to fields in the table, as well as methods that correspond to database transactions, such as save, delete, and various lookup options:

```
$post->title = 'Post Title';

$post->body = 'Post body content';

$post->save();
```

Almost all of our models will be the ancestors of the CActiveRecord class.

In the Yii blog demo, if we look at the Post model, we will see that it contains rules for each field based on the database constraints. It knows which fields are integer or text-based, as well as length and null requirements. These control the validations Yii will perform when attempting to save records.

```
/* protected/models/Post.php */
public function rules()
{
    // NOTE: you should only define rules for those
    //attributes that will receive user inputs.
    return array(
        array('title, content, status', 'required'),
        array('status', 'in', 'range'=>array(1,2,3)),
```

```
                    array('title', 'length', 'max'=>128),
                    array('tags', 'match',
                        'pattern'=>'/^[\w\s,]+$/',
                        'message'=>'Tags can only contain word characters.'),
                    array('tags', 'normalizeTags'),
                    array('title, status', 'safe', 'on'=>'search'),
                );
        }
```

Another important thing that Yii will set up based on the database table is any foreign key relationship it finds. For the blog demo, a post will have a single author that it belongs to and a number of comments that belong to the Post. As we can see in the following example, these relationships can be quite sophisticated. Just have a look at the official documentation for the CActiveRecord.relations method (http://www.yiiframework.com/doc/api/1.1/ CActiveRecord#relations-detail). The comments have been filtered to only show approved comments and to retrieve comments with a particular sort order. Yii also allows statistical relationships, so you can get a count of related items such as the count of all the approved comments:

```
        public function relations()
        {
            // NOTE: you may need to adjust the relation name and the related
            // class name for the relations automatically generated below.
            return array(
                'author' => array(self::BELONGS_TO, 'User', 'author_id'),
                'comments' => array(self::HAS_MANY, 'Comment', 'post_id',
                    'condition'=>'comments.status='.Comment::STATUS_APPROVED,
                    'order'=>'comments.create_timeDESC'),
                'commentCount' => array(self::STAT, 'Comment', 'post_id',
                    'condition'=>'status='.Comment::STATUS_APPROVED),
            );
        }
```

Beyond rules and relationships, the model defaults to having a section for user-friendly labels for attributes, which default to being only slightly cleaner than the actual table names, but can be changed to fit your application needs:

```
        public function attributeLabels()
        {
            return array(
                'id' => 'Id',
                'title' => 'Title',
                'content' => 'Content',
                'tags' => 'Tags',
                'status' => 'Status',
```

```
        'create_time' => 'Create Time',
        'update_time' => 'Update Time',
        'author_id' => 'Author',
    );
}
```

There is also a search method, which is intended for use on list pages.

Please note that this method is not important to the functionality of the model per se; it is just a helper method. It returns an instance of CDataProvider, which is used by virtually all list and table widgets in Yii; so, the authors of the framework decided to include this method in the model being autogenerated to further reduce the need to write scaffolding code. The developer can decide to feed hand crafted data providers to the widgets or instead use some other helpers.

Yii has widgets for displaying and paging through records, such as CGridView or CListView. These will use the search method to create a data provider object for this interaction. Again, you can customize the behavior of the way records are retrieved with this method. The Post model has been set to add some default sorting options and ignore some fields:

```
public function search()
{
    $criteria=new CDbCriteria;
    $criteria->compare('title',$this->title,true);
    $criteria->compare('status',$this->status);
    return new CActiveDataProvider('Post', array(
        'criteria'=>$criteria,
        'sort'=>array(
            'defaultOrder'=>'status, update_time DESC',
        ),
    ));
}
```

Controllers

The job of a controller is to deal with incoming requests, identify the appropriate action method, and ultimately render a view to return to the user. When a request comes in to Yii, the URL dictates which controller and action has been called for. All requests are first handled by the index.php file in the root of your website. This file starts loading your application by instantiating Yii and referencing your configuration file. It then looks at the rest of the URL to determine which controller should run. There is a route parameter r that is checked. The appropriate use is index.php?r=controller/action.

By default, applications generated by the ./yiic webapp console tool have a SiteController controller, which handles standard actions such as presenting a default homepage or dealing with login/logout actions. This controller will be called when you bring up your app without any URL parameters.

If we elaborate on that, then what is really happening is that when Yii gets a request without a controller specified, it will forward this request to the controller whose name is set in the `defaultController` configuration parameter (see `http://www.yiiframework.com/doc/api/1.1/CWebApplication#defaultController-detail`), and it's default value is `site`.

As you probably guessed already, if the request doesn't specify the action, then the `defaultAction` will be called. Of course, it's defined not as the global configuration parameter but separately in each controller as its class property (see `http://www.yiiframework.com/doc/api/1.1/CController#defaultAction-detail`). The default value for the `defaultAction` property is `index`.

So, since site/index is the default behavior when no `r` parameter is given, going to `www.yoursite.com` is the equivalent of going to `www.yoursite.com/index.php?r=site/index`. By default, with a model such as `Post`, you would expect to see routes like this:

- `www.yoursite.com/index.php?r=post/index`
- `www.yoursite.com/index.php?r=post/create`

...and so on.

You can see that the actual blog demo does not follow this pattern though. Instead, its paths look like `www.yoursite.com/posts` and `www.yoursite.com/post/create`. Ultimately, you can make any kind of custom URLs with Yii. Later in this book, we will look at ways to change the way your URL looks, which are cleaner, but still resolve to the same thing.

If you take a look at one of your controller files in `protected/controllers/`, you will see that it has a number of methods that look like: `actionCreate`, `actionIndex`, `actionUpdate`, and so on. The second half of these names correspond to the action that would be in the URL. For example, in `PostController`, `actionCreate` corresponds to the URL `index.php?r=post/create`. The view and update actions expect an additional parameter for the ID of the specified entity. By default, this URL would look like `index.php?r=post/view&id=1`, where 1 is the primary key ID of a single post.

All of this means that `actionLogin`, `actionLogout`, and other actions generated for you by Gii in `SiteController` are just example scaffolding, and if you need to, you can make a completely different structure of controllers and actions.

To better understand how these actions work, let us examine a couple of actions in detail. For most entities, one of the simplest actions is to view a single item, because it does only one thing, which is to respond to GET requests and show the view template. Other actions are more complicated due to the fact they can respond to GET or POST actions. For example, update will simply return the form if the method is GET, but when you post data to this same action, it attempts to save the item and redirect you to the view screen.

```
public function actionView($id)
{
    $model=$this->loadModel($id);
```

```
    $this->render('view',array(
        'model'=>$model,
    ));
}
```

What the preceding code does is that it starts by running the `loadModel()` method, which is found at the bottom of the controller code. This method looks for a URL parameter called `id` and does a lookup using ActiveRecord methods. It throws the 404 exception if it fails to find a corresponding record, which is appropriate since 404 is generally used for Page-Not-Found situations:

```
public function loadModel($id)
{
    $model=Post::model()->findByPk($id);
    if($model===null)
        throw new CHttpException(
            404,
            'The requested page does not exist.'
        );
    return $model;
}
```

If a model is found, the action method continues and all it has left to do is pass that model on to the view with the render function:

```
public function actionUpdate($id)
{
    $model=$this->loadModel($id);

    if (isset($_POST['Post']))
    {
        $model->attributes=$_POST['Post'];
        if ($model->save())
            $this->redirect(array('view','id'=>$model->id));
    }

    $this->render('update',array(
        'model'=>$model,
    ));
}
```

The Update action, unlike View, does two things. It will respond to both HTTP GET and POST requests. The middle section of the function pertains only to the condition of receiving a POST, so it will be skipped over. In the case of a regular GET, this looks identical to how the View behaves; it simply loads the model based on an expected ID parameter and renders a view file with that model. The interesting part is when you post the form contained on the Update view back to this action. In that case, the old model state is loaded, then its attributes are overwritten with values from the $_POST array, which contains the form body from the HTML. On the condition that this saves without violating any validation or rules set in the model class, the request is then forwarded to the View page, so see the newly-saved version of the item. If for some reason the save method fails, the code will fall through and render the Update form again. The only difference here is that since the model failed to save, it now contains information about the reasons why it has failed. $model->getErrors() will return an array of problems that prevented the save from succeeding. When the Update form is rendered again, these errors will appear at the top of the form, making it simple for the user to correct their mistakes.

Views

Yii's views are typically put together with at least two parts. There is a main site layout.php view, which is a wrapper for different views when the controller's render method is called. The benefit of this is that your overall site design is contained in one place and individual views only need to consist of the relevant content for the body of the page. You can also have more than one standard layout such as a two or a three column format. You can also have a layout included in another layout, by means of the beginContent method; see http://www.yiiframework.com/doc/api/1.1/CBaseController#beginContent-detail. You'll find the layout file in views/layouts. You can also have a different layout assigned to different controllers; see http://www.yiiframework.com/doc/api/1.1/CController#layout-detail. All other views should be contained within a folder that corresponds to the controller they belong to. By default, there are just two folders: layouts and site. For each additional model, your CRUD will create another folder.

Recap

At this point, we have talked about our database design and how to automatically generate ActiveRecord models for each of our important or entity-class tables. Then, we created controllers and views with the CRUD generator. At this point, we should have a basic database interface. Unfortunately, that's not quite a full-blown web application, because we are not writing the user interface for database administration here, but instead we are building a blog. We'll cover a lot of great features further on in this book, but one more really important step in getting started is to alter the authentication process to use your actual users table/model.

User authentication

Now that the database is configured, one of the first steps you'll want to take is to make the site use your users table for authentication. The control for this is contained within the file `protected/components/UserIdentity.php`. By default, this file has two hard-coded user account/password combinations. Replace the content of this file with the following code:

```php
<?php
class UserIdentity extends CUserIdentity
{
    private $_id;

    public function authenticate()
    {
        $username=strtolower($this->username);
        $user=User::model()->find(
            'LOWER(username)=?',
            array($username)
        );
        if($user===null)
            $this->errorCode=self::ERROR_USERNAME_INVALID;
        else if(!$user->validatePassword($this->password))
            $this->errorCode=self::ERROR_PASSWORD_INVALID;
        else
        {
            $this->_id=$user->id;
            $this->username=$user->username;
            $this->errorCode=self::ERROR_NONE;
        }
        return $this->errorCode==self::ERROR_NONE;
    }

    public function getId()
    {
        return $this->_id;
    }
}
```

What you see in here is pretty standard code to authenticate users by login/password pairs stored in the database. If you follow the code, which is intimidating only at first glance, you see that it does the following:

1. Tries to find in the DB the record about user having the username specified.

2. If no user with this username is recorded, it sets the error code to `ERROR_USERNAME_INVALID` and proceeds to the end of the procedure.

3. If the user exists, validate password specified using whichever method is defined for validation in the user model.

4. If validation is unsuccessful, set error code to `ERROR_PASSWORD_INVALID` and proceed to the end of the procedure.

5. If validation is successful, set the error code to `ERROR_NONE` and proceed to the end of the procedure.

6. The user is authenticated if the error code is `ERROR_NONE`.

Note the highlighted line in the code. It means that we need to modify the user model as well. Put the two following functions into it:

```
public function validatePassword($password)
{
    return crypt($password, $this->password)===$this->password;
}

public function hashPassword($password)
{
    return crypt($password, $this->generateSalt());
}
```

The function named `validatePassword`, as we already saw, was used in the authentication process. The function named `hashPassword` should be used when the new user model is saved to the database.

The idea is as follows: we do not store whole passwords as plain text. We hash them using the built-in PHP function `crypt` and store these hashes instead. The implementation of `crypt` has a very important and useful property. When we pass it the desired password as the first argument, and the already made hash of the same password as the second argument (which is the *salt* of the encryption), it produces the same hash as provided as the second argument. This property is exactly what is used in the `validatePassword()` function.

OK, now about what is the salt. For our purposes, you can just think of salt as a special string that tells `crypt` how exactly to encrypt the string provided. The exact rules are written in the official PHP documentation for `crypt`, accessible on the website here: http://www.php.net/manual/en/function.crypt.php.

So, there's still a `generateSalt` function that needs to be implemented. You can just use the following implementation verbatim:

```
/**
 * Generate a random salt in the crypt(3) standard Blowfish format.
 *
 * @param int $cost Cost parameter from 4 to 31.
 *
```

```php
 * @throws Exception on invalid cost parameter.
 * @return string A Blowfish hash salt for use in PHP's crypt()
 */
private function generateSalt($cost = 13)
{
    if (!is_numeric($cost) || $cost < 4 || $cost > 31) {
        throw new Exception(
            "cost parameter must be between 4 and 31"
        );
    }
    $rand = array();
    for ($i = 0; $i < 8; $i += 1) {
        $rand[] = pack('S', mt_rand(0, 0xffff));
    }
    $rand[] = substr(microtime(), 2, 6);
    $rand = sha1(implode('', $rand), true);
    $salt = '$2a$' . sprintf('%02d', $cost) . '$';
    $salt .= strtr(
        substr(base64_encode($rand), 0, 22),
        array('+' => '.')
    );
    return $salt;
}
```

This way you have the complete implementation of user authentication made using the current best practices in this field.

You should note, though, the precise reasons for this implementation.

First of all, we don't store the passwords as the user entered them. This is a security precaution in case the password database will be accessed by a malicious user.

Secondly, we use a pretty hardcore Blowfish algorithm, which is very, very slow to run. This is a second precaution in case the malicious user tries to guess the passwords using brute force, for example, encrypting some arbitrary strings the same way we did and comparing the result with the values in our database. If we used something fast, such as the MD5 algorithm, then it would be a lot easier on modern high-performance hardware.

You probably want to look at the detailed description of what's going on here on the relevant tutorial at the Yii website. This particular authentication scheme is described on the blog demo at **Initial Prototyping | Authenticating User**. The direct URL is http://www.yiiframework.com/doc/blog/1.1/en/prototype.auth.

Top 5 features you need to know about

As we saw in the previous section, it's easy to quickly set up forms and views for the basic CRUD operations. However, if you look more closely, you'll find that every form element is either a text box or a text area. That's fine for fields such as `Title` and `Body`, but not for other things such as foreign key relationships, date fields, and values for which you might want to use a more specialized widget, such as a slider. These alternative input choices are vital, because you obviously can't expect your users to set something like the category ID for a post by knowing the primary key of the category they want, or the exact date format you want to use.

Basic security considerations

For displaying user data, run it through the `CHtmlPurifier` filter:

```php
<?php $this->beginWidget('CHtmlPurifier'); ?>
<?php echo $model->content; ?>
<?php $this->endWidget(); ?>
```

When receiving user input, the easiest way to use it on a single field is illustrated as follows, and we will revisit this topic in the following section:

```php
$p = new CHtmlPurifier();
$model->content = $p->purify($_POST['Model']['content']);
```

The CSRF option goes into the components section of the `main.php` config file:

```php
//protected/config/main.php
'components'=>array(
  'request'=>array(
    'enableCsrfValidation'=>true,
  ),
);
```

Form components – CHtml, CActiveForm, and Zii

`CHtml` is the basic helper class to output HTML tags. `CActiveForm` was added later to make it even easier to set up forms and bind model properties to input elements. Additionally, `CHtml` and `CActiveForm` contain a number of useful helper functions. Zii is a set of widgets for things such as menus, lists, and grid elements. Zii also provides wrappers for jQuery UI widgets such as Accordion, DatePicker, ProgressBar, Slider, Tabs, and so on. Let's take a look at how we can use these items to enhance CRUD forms.

The core form created by the CRUD generator (`_form.php`) will be used by both the Create and Update actions. In the `views/{controller}/` directory, you will find `create.php`, `update.php`, and `_form.php`. The Create and Update actions render `create.php` and `update.php` respectively, but what you will notice is that each of these is really just a wrapper for `_form.php`. Inside, they both contain a `renderPartial()` call, which pass the model to the `_form.php` view.

Whereas `render()` incorporates the site layout, `renderPartial()` only produces the content of the specified template.

This is something to keep in mind while building your forms. You can use `renderPartial` to separate out pieces of templates should you need to reuse them in multiple views, or if you wish to reduce the size of your individual view files.

Another useful tip when working with `_form.php` is to know whether or not you are on the Create or Update view. This determination can be easily made by checking the model property `isNewRecord`, as you will find they have done with the form submit button. This button will display different text based on whether you are adding a new item or saving changes to an existing one.

```
echo CHtml::submitButton($model->isNewRecord ? 'Create' : 'Save');
```

So, let's say we have a simple blog system. Our posts only have `Title` and `Content` objects, but then we might also want a foreign key relationship to a category entity. The category CRUD form is simple if we only want a category name (and a primary key ID for referencing). This form will be generated ready to go out of the box, because all we need is a single text box for a category name. The heart of the category form would look like this:

```
<div class="row">
<?php
    echo $form->labelEx($model,'name');
    echo $form->textField(
        $model, 'name',
        array('size'=>60,'maxlength'=>90)
    );
    echo $form->error($model,'name');
?>
</div>

<div class="row buttons">
<?php
    echo CHtml::submitButton(
        $model->isNewRecord ? 'Create' : 'Save'
    );
?>
</div>
```

Yii is smart enough to know that a primary key doesn't show up as a form element, so there's only one field in the form. We can use this CRUD immediately to populate a few categories for use on the POST form.

Moving on to the POST form, we'll probably want to use an HTML select element for this, unless there are only two or three, where radio buttons might make more sense.

Here's what the POST form looks like by default:

```php
<div class="row">
<?php
    echo $form->labelEx($model,'category_id');
    echo $form->textField($model,'category_id');
    echo $form->error($model,'category_id');
?>
</div>

<div class="row">
<?php
    echo $form->labelEx($model,'title');
    echo $form->textField(
        $model, 'title',
        array('size'=>60,'maxlength'=>120)
    );
    echo $form->error($model,'title');
?>
</div>

<div class="row">
<?php
    echo $form->labelEx($model,'cotent');
    echo $form->textArea(
        $model, 'content',
        array('rows'=>6, 'cols'=>50)
    );
    echo $form->error($model,'content');
?>
</div>

<div class="row buttons">
<?php
    echo CHtml::submitButton(
        $model->isNewRecord ? 'Create' : 'Save'
    );
?>
</div>
```

Notice how the first row is only using `textField` for category ID (`category_id`). This is what we want to fix.

You can use `CHtml` or `CActiveForm` to accomplish this, but as long as the option is available in `CActiveForm`, that is what we should use. The change is simple. In essence, all you need to do is swap `$form->textField` with `$form->dropDownList`. However, that's not quite enough. A drop-down list requires just a little bit more information. It would be safe enough for Yii to assume you want the primary key of the related model, but it has no way to know what field is the actual display field. Here's where we use one of the static `CHtml` helper methods to set up an associated array of keys and values to be used in the building of the select options.

The final product looks like the following code:

```php
<?php
    echo $form->dropDownList(
        $model, 'category_id',
        CHtml::listData(
            Category::model()->findAll(),
            'id', 'name'
        )
    );
?>
```

`CHtml::listData` expects an array of models. It doesn't matter how this is retrieved. If you need to filter these items, you may do so before passing the final result to this call. The next two parameters are the key and display values to be used for each option.

Now, the form should show a nice, clean select box showing all the available categories:

Home » Posts » **Create**

Create Post

*Fields with * are required.*

Category *
[Sports ▼]

Title *
[ ]

Body
[ ]

[Create]

For the sake of argument, let's assume our posts can have a publish date field that we might use to prevent items from showing up on the list until the desired date. By default, this would show up as `textField`, just like the category ID. Replacing it with the Zii wrapper of the jQuery UI DatePicker, aptly named `CJuiDatePicker`, would look like the following code:

```
// replace this:
<?php echo $form->textField($model, 'publish_date'); ?>

// with this:
<?php $this->widget('zii.widgets.jui.CJuiDatePicker',array(
        'model'=>$model,
        'attribute'=>'publish_date',
        'options'=>array(
            'showAnim'=>'fold',
        ),
        'htmlOptions'=>array(
            'style'=>'height:20px;'
        ),
    )); ?>
```

If you want to follow the ActiveForm style, you must specify the `model` and `attribute` options as shown in the preceding code. To simply pass a date value with your form, replace the model and attribute with a name value that will correspond to the input name.

Unfortunately, we're not quite done with the `date` field here. Dates are always a tricky subject on the web. Odds are, the default format that the picker gives you isn't the way your database will want to store it, or maybe it's not the display style desired for your applications. In most cases, you will need to address this on the server side when receiving posted values and when pushing dates out.

As far as displaying different date formats, this can easily be handled by adding the `dateFormat` element to the options array. For example, the default would be `03/16/2013` (the day this sentence was written). The date format for this is `mm/dd/yy`. If you don't want two column values for single digits and just the last two digits for the year, use `m/d/y`. Or, if you want something that looks like the MySQL date format, use `yy-mm-dd`. That will take care of the value you see when selecting something from the picker.

The specification that Yii uses for date formats is described here: `http://www.unicode.org/reports/tr35/tr35-dates.html#Date_Format_Patterns`. This is mentioned in the documentation for the `CDateFormatter` class.

However, two problems remain.

If you're not following the exact MySQL format, you'll want to reformat the date on the server side after a post. You would want to do this anyway, just to be safe, since users can still type in the field and post their own values.

There are two places where this will need to be addressed, because this form can be posted in two different ways, as discussed before—on Create and Update, so the date translation will have to be added to `actionCreate` and `actionUpdate`. In either case, the code is the same. After you get into the `if(isset($_POST)){}` block, you can expect this field might be filled out.

Use the PHP `date` function along with the string-to-time function to fix whatever value you received:

```
if (isset($_POST['Post2']))
{
    $model->attributes=$_POST['Post2'];
    $model->publish_date = date(
        'Y-m-d',
        strtotime($model->publish_date)
    );
    if($model->save())
        $this->redirect(array('view','id'=>$model->id));
}
```

The second issue with dates that you will need to address is relevant on any views that show this field. This could be the update form, where you would want the field prepopulated with the display style date format, or the view and list screens. The easiest way to address this is to change it before you render the views. For example, the View action looks like this by default:

```
public function actionView($id)
{
    $this->render('view',array(
        'model'=>$this->loadModel($id),
    ));
}
```

We'll need to change the model before calling the render method, so we have to rearrange this a little bit while adding our date format fix. Something like this should do the trick:

```
public function actionView($id)
{
    $model = $this->loadModel($id);
    $model->publish_date = date('m/d/Y', strtotime($model->publish_
date));
    $this->render('view',array(
        'model'=>$model,
    ));
}
```

This is essentially the same process we did for saving the posted value, just in reverse.

Note that you can put this logic for reformatting the date on a deeper level into the model code. Each Yii model has a pair of special methods, `afterFind` and `beforeSave`, which are fired by Yii automatically right after the model is populated with data from the database or just before saving the updated data to the database respectively. Utilizing these methods, you will not need to modify the `actionView` method at all, instead you'll need to add the following to the code of your post model:

```
/**
 * For displaying the model on pages,
 * we convert publishing date to 'MM/DD/YYYY' format.
 */
public function afterFind()
{
    $this->publish_date = date('m/d/Y', strtotime($this->publish_
date));
}


/**
 * Publish date of Post is being stored in the MySQL in 'YYYY-MM-DD'
format.
 */
public function beforeSave()
{
    $this->publish_date = date(
        'Y-m-d',
        strtotime($this->publish_date)
    );
}
```

Of course, this has a catch. After you set up these two handlers, you will always convert your dates, even if you don't want or need to. When the conversion is at the hands of a controller, it can decide whether or not to do it.

Adding custom views

Now that we've covered the basics of how the CRUD forms work, it's time to take a look at building more specialized interfaces. Unless you're strictly making a database application, odds are the basic CRUD functionality isn't going to be enough. There are a couple of ways to go about this. Every page needs to be an action within a controller, but controllers do not need to be tied specifically into a specific model. Whether or not you work within an existing controller or not depends on whether the new view really applies to an entity.

For example, if you allow users to submit posts that enter a pending state and must be approved by an administrator before being published, you might want a page that lists these pending posts and that has buttons for viewing and approving them. Something like this makes sense to keep within the `PostController`.

There are a few things to cover before we dig too far into this process. If we're adding an approved field to our Post model, it will show up on the _form.php file by default. We will want to hide it from non-administrator users, as well as use a checkbox input element instead of the text field it will insert by default. Since we haven't yet talked about using proper user access roles, we will rely on the standard Yii user accounts for permissions on this field. Later in this section, we will return to this example with proper role-based access checking.

In MySQL, you can set up the approved field as approved tinyint(1) default 0. That way, when not showing this field to non-administrator users, the posts will default to 0 (unapproved). Also, when changing the input field to a checkbox, it will work with values of 0 and 1.

```php
<?php
//quick and dirty hide for non-admin users
if (Yii::app()->user->name == 'admin') {
    echo CHtml::openTag('div', array('class' => 'row'));
        echo $form->labelEx($model,'approved');
        echo $form->checkBox($model,'approved');
        echo $form->error($model,'approved');
    echo CHtml::closeTag('div');
}
?>
```

By default, PostController contains an index page, which is a general, pageable list. To create a page that only deals with a particular type of post, we start by adding a new action to the PostController. Assuming our Post model also contains an approved property, we can use this to generate a filtered list of models to pass to the a pending view template.

In PostController, if we want this list to look like the index list but with a filter, the easiest thing to do is to copy the index action, rename it, and add some filtering. We can even use the same view script, but it's best to copy this over as well. So, protected/views/post/index.php should be copied to protected/views/post/pending.php. These views have breadcrumb and menu options that you may wish to have look different, so it makes the most sense to keep these files different.

```php
public function actionPending()
{
    $dataProvider=new CActiveDataProvider('Post');
    $criteria = new CDbCriteria;
    $criteria->condition = 'approved=0';
    $dataProvider->criteria = $criteria;
    $this->render('pending',array(
        'dataProvider'=>$dataProvider,
    ));
}
```

The view template, in this case, is making use of a Zii widget called CListView, which makes use of CActiveDataProvider to get relevant models and to handle things like paging automatically. On the view template, it looks like this:

```
<?php $this->widget('zii.widgets.CListView', array(
  'dataProvider'=>$dataProvider,
  'itemView'=>'_view',
)); ?>
```

Each item is then rendered via the _view.php template, which can be altered or duplicated to fit the needs of each different content type. By default, Yii views are very plain and generally only list properties in rows or tables. Even the actual view.php template, which is used by actionView to show a single entity, merely displays each field in an HTML table.

For listing rows of records with action buttons, the admin interface has a much better display. Instead of CListView, it uses CGridView. It also provides the ability to search on fields (columns in the display table), as well as possessing a more sophisticated advanced search form.

```
Yii::app()->clientScript->registerScript('search', "
$('.search-button').click(function(){
    $('.search-form').toggle();
    return false;
});
$('.search-form form').submit(function(){
    $('#post-grid').yiiGridView('update', {
        data: $(this).serialize()
    });
    return false;
});
");
?>


<h1>Manage Posts</h1>


<p>
You may optionally enter a comparison operator (<b>&lt;</b>,
<b>&lt;=</b>, <b>&gt;</b>, <b>&gt;=</b>, <b>&lt;&gt;</b>
or <b>=</b>) at the beginning of each of your search values to specify
how the comparison should be done.
</p>

<?php echo CHtml::link('Advanced Search','#',array('class'=>'search-
button')); ?>
<div class="search-form" style="display:none">
<?php $this->renderPartial('_search',array(
  'model'=>$model,
```

```
)); ?>
</div><!-- search-form -->

<?php $this->widget('zii.widgets.grid.CGridView', array(
    'id'=>'post-grid',
    'dataProvider'=>$model->search(),
    'filter'=>$model,
    'columns'=>array(
        'id',
        'cat_id',
        'title',
        'body',
        'approved',
        array(
            'class'=>'CButtonColumn',
        ),
    ),
)); ?>
```

Let's assume you're not concerned with the advanced search for the pending posts view. We can copy the `admin.php` script over to `pending.php` (instead of copying `index.php` to `pending.php` as mentioned previously). This action uses the `$model->search()` method to get the DataProvider for this widget. For now, we can ignore that piece. We'll return to it later.

One thing to notice here in the `CGridView` widget is the columns list. You can choose which fields you want to have display. In a lot of cases, you might not want to show all the fields, or you may want them to show up differently. If the actual Post ID is not important, we can remove that item. Since category ID, as a number, doesn't tell us much, we can easily make that show the name field for the given ID. Another thing we're going to want to change is the last column. `CButtonColumn` defaults to giving us three buttons: `view`, `update`, and `delete`. The form we're trying to build is intended to allow an administrator to approve pending posts, so we really need an action button for doing the approving. We might also have this as an option in other places too, such as the view and update screens, so it might make sense to leave those buttons there. In any case, we must customize both the `CGridView` column list as well as `CButtonColumn` itself.

```
<?php $this->widget('zii.widgets.grid.CGridView', array(
    'id'=>'post-pending-grid',
    'dataProvider'=>$model->search(),
    'columns'=>array(
        array(
            'name'=>'cat_id',
            'value'=>'$data->category->name',
        ),
        'title',
```

```
      array(
        'class'=>'CButtonColumn',
        'template'=>'{approve} {view} {update} {delete}',
        'buttons'=>array(
          'approve' => array(
            'url'=>'', //need to set this
            'imageUrl'=>Yii::app()->request->baseUrl
              .'/images/approve.png',
          ),
        ),
      ),
    ),
  )); ?>
```

The highlighted lines are what's most important here. The `buttons` property tells the widget what buttons, to generate for this grid. In here, we have the `approve` button defined manually. You have three buttons, `update`, `view`, and `delete`, for free with any `CGridView`. The `template` property tells the widget in what order and what buttons to render. So, if you configure some custom buttons, as we did with `approve`, then you have to mention it in the `template` property. A full description of what parameters can be defined for each button can be found in the documentation for the `CButtonColumn.buttons` property at `http://www.yiiframework.com/doc/api/1.1/CButtonColumn#buttons-detail`.

Note that we still need to properly configure the `url` property for our `approve` button.

Let's do the AJAX update for when a user clicks on the approve button. It will send a request to the `/post/approve` endpoint, which we will create shortly, and update the grid afterwards. Here's how we do it:

```
'buttons'=>array(
    'approve' => array(
        'imageUrl'=>Yii::app()->request->baseUrl.'/images/approve.
png',
        'url'=>'Yii::app()->createUrl("post/approve",
array("id"=>$data->id))',
      'options' => array(
          'ajax' => array(
              'type' => 'post',
              'url'=>'js:$(this).attr("href")',
              'success' => 'js:function(data) { $("#post-pending-
grid"). yiiGridView('update'); }'
          )),
    ),
),
```

After that, we write the simplest possible endpoint in our `PostController`:

```
public function actionApprove($id)
{
    $model= Post::model()->findByPk($id);
    if (!$model)
        throw new CHttpException(404);

    $model->approved = 1;
    $model->save();
}
```

This just changes the approved status of the Post to `true` value and saves it. Note the common practice of checking whether we got the correct Post ID and throwing an exception if not.

For listing pending posts, we do the following:

```
public function actionPending()
{
    $model=new Post('search');
    $model->unsetAttributes();  // clear any default values
    $model->approved = 0;
    if(isset($_GET['Post']))
        $model->attributes=$_GET['Post'];

    $this->render('pending',array(
        'model'=>$model,
    ));
}
```

This table will only show the post category by name and the title of the post. After you set the `approved` field to zero in this particular model instance, it'll be used as a filter for the grid view.

Extensions

Another great feature of Yii, and the Yii community, is the library of user-contributed extensions that you will find on the Yii website (`http://www.yiiframework.com/extensions/`). There are currently over 1,100 extensions that make it easy to drop in specialized functionality. Extension categories include Authorization, Caching, Date and Time, File System, Mail, Security, User Interface, Validation, and a few others. In this section, we'll take a look at a couple of really good ones.

TinyMCE

The most popular extension by far is **tinymce**. This, as you might have guessed, is a wrapper for the **TinyMCE** (http://www.tinymce.com/) WYSIWYG editor. It attaches to a text area input and provides a toggle between the HTML view and a Preview mode, where styles appear as they would when published. Users are given controls, such as font selection/color, text alignment, bold/italic/underline, and so on.

To use the TinyMCE extension, you first download and extract it into the protected/ extensions directory. After that, simply replace the single line of _form.php that normally calls for textArea with the following, which will yield the full set of controls:

```php
<?php $this->widget('application.extensions.tinymce.ETinyMce', array(
        'model'=>$model,
        'attribute'=>'content',
        'editorTemplate'=>'full',
        'htmlOptions'=>array('rows'=>6, 'cols'=>50,
'class'=>'tinymce')
)); ?>
```

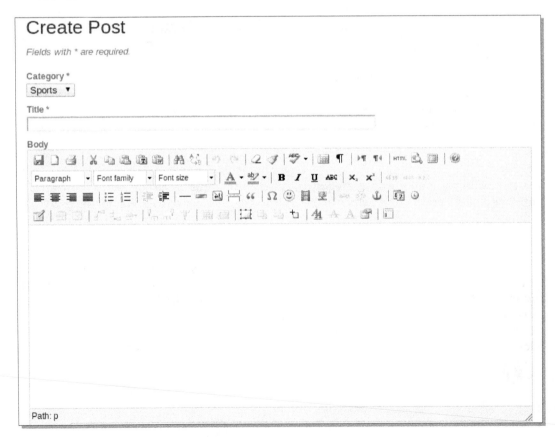

MbMenu

Another very sought after feature on most websites today is drop-down menus. **MbMenu** provides an extension to the default Yii CMenu class, making it easy to plug in for existing projects. To get started, again, all you have to do is download and extract the extension into the `protected/extensions` folder. The main site menu is configured in `protected/views/layout/main.php`, so that is where we must go to make our changes.

By default, the menu looks like this:

```
<div id="mainmenu">
  <?php $this->widget('zii.widgets.CMenu',array(
    'items'=>array(
      array(
        'label'=>'Home',
        'url'=>array('/site/index')
      ),
      array(
        'label'=>'About',
        'url'=>array('/site/page', 'view'=>'about')
      ),
      array(
        'label'=>'Contact',
        'url'=>array('/site/contact')
      ),
      array(
        'label'=>'Login',
        'url'=>array('/site/login'),
        'visible'=>Yii::app()->user->isGuest
      ),
      array(
        'label'=>'Logout ('.Yii::app()->user->name.')',
        'url'=>array('/site/logout'),
        'visible'=>!Yii::app()->user->isGuest
      )
    ),
  )); ?>
</div><!-- mainmenu -->
```

To use MbMenu, we must change the widget to `application.extensions.mbmenu.MbMenu`. Then we may nest arrays of items within individual menu items following the same format CMenu used by default. Going with our example, we might want to first add a menu item for posts that links to the post index list. With the old CMenu way, we would just do this:

```
<div id="mainmenu">
  <?php $this->widget('zii.widgets.CMenu',array(
    'items'=>array(
```

```php
      array(
        'label'=>'Home',
        'url'=>array('/site/index')
      ),
      array(
        'label'=>'Posts',
        'url'=>array('/post/index')
      ),
      array(
        'label'=>'About',
        'url'=>array('/site/page', 'view'=>'about')
      ),
      array(
        'label'=>'Contact',
        'url'=>array('/site/contact')
      ),
      array(
        'label'=>'Login',
        'url'=>array('/site/login'),
        'visible'=>Yii::app()->user->isGuest
      ),
      array(
        'label'=>'Logout ('.Yii::app()->user->name.')',
        'url'=>array('/site/logout'),
        'visible'=>!Yii::app()->user->isGuest
      )
    ),
  )); ?>
</div><!-- mainmenu -->
```

Now, let's say we want to add some of the CRUD actions and the pending list as submenu items. That would look like the following:

```php
<div id="mainMbMenu">
<?php
  $this->widget('application.extensions.mbmenu.MbMenu', array(
    'items'=>array(
      array(
        'label'=>'Home',
        'url'=>array('/site/index')
      ),
      array(
        'label'=>'Posts',
        'url'=>array('/post/index'),
        'items'=>array(
```

```
    array(
      'label'=>'All Posts',
      'url'=>array('/post/index')
    ),
    array(
      'label'=>'Add Post',
      'url'=>array('/post/create'),
      'visible'=>!Yii::app()->user->isGuest
    ),
    array(
      'label'=>'Pending',
      'url'=>array('/post/pending'),
      'visible'=>Yii::app()->user->name=='admin'
    ),
  ),
),
array(
  'label'=>'About',
  'url'=>array('/site/page', 'view'=>'about')
),
array(
  'label'=>'Contact',
  'url'=>array('/site/contact')
),
array(
  'label'=>'Login',
  'url'=>array('/site/login'),
  'visible'=>Yii::app()->user->isGuest
),
array(
  'label'=>'Logout ('.Yii::app()->user->name.')',
  'url'=>array('/site/logout'),
  'visible'=>!Yii::app()->user->isGuest
)
  ),
)); ?>
</div><!-- mainmenu -->
```

Note that this widget has its own CSS, so the ID of the wrapper div element should be changed from mainmenu to mainMbMenu. Also, we don't want non-admin users to see the menu option for the pending list or non-authenticated users to see the link to create a post, so we have to specify the visible condition.

Yii-User and Yii-User-Management

These two extensions are among the most downloaded extensions. **Yii-User** provides mechanisms for user registrations and all the issues that arise with that process, such as confirming e-mail, resetting passwords, and user profiles. **Yii-User-Management** provides many more of the same features, but additionally includes groups, inter-user messaging, and user roles.

Yii-Shop

Yii-Shop is a fully-featured, internationalized shopping cart extension. It handles different types of products with variations, tax calculations, shipping and payment methods, as well as invoicing and delivery slips.

Cal

This is a great jQuery-based calendar extension. Use it to create and schedule events that display on a full-sized calendar.

Fancybox

Who doesn't like those modal pop-up image viewers? This one is perfect for fancy looking image galleries. It's a wrapper around the third-party application **Fancybox,** located at `http://fancyapps.com/fancybox/`.

Other great extensions

There are so many great extensions available for Yii, and for the most part, they are as easy to drop in and use as the two examples illustrated earlier. In the next section, we'll be talking about another great extension that makes it easy to deal with one of the most important issues in web-based applications, namely access permissions.

Role-based access control

A common practice in software applications for decades has been to assign permissions for specific actions to generalized roles. Users can be granted one or more roles, through which they will be enabled to perform certain functions. Given the blog example, general registered users might be given a role like visitor. That role would be linked to a limited set of possible actions. For instance, visitors might only be allowed to create comments for posts, but not posts themselves. Another role might be given to a select number of users who are actually allowed to create posts. This might be called **post creator**. Roles often describe the intended behavior, and even if they are never publicly visible as part of the site, they serve to keep things simple on the administrative or programmatic side of things. A final, top-level role might be something like admin, which would probably handle things like enabling new users or approving posts. All-in-all, this process of granting permission for certain actions to user roles is known as **role-based access control (RBAC)**, and it is very important in Yii.

SRBAC

One of the easiest ways to get going with role based access controls is this widely popular extension called **SRBAC** (`http://www.yiiframework.com/doc/guide/1.1/en/basics.module`). This extension provides a graphical interface for configuring roles, tasks, and operations. Operations are assigned to tasks, tasks are assigned to roles, and finally, roles are assigned to users. At the lowest level, operations are a one-to-one mapping to an action. For example, viewing a post is `actionView` in the post controller. `PostView` is the operation that would be created to map to this action. Similarly, operations would be created for all actions in the `PostController`. By default, SRBAC will also set up two tasks for each controller. For Post, these would be `PostViewing` and `PostAdministrating`. View and Index are read-only operations, so they generally get lumped into `PostViewing`, whereas Create, Update, Delete, and Admin fit more reasonably in `PostAdministering`. You can always reserve administering for a few more important tasks, such as Delete or just Admin, but you'll probably want to create another task like `PostCreating` to fit in-between strictly view-only and actual creation/editing of content.

To make use of SRBAC with a particular controller, there are a few changes that need to be made. First, we must configure this extension, which is a slightly different process from the earlier examples. This is an older extension that follows a less used pattern for install. Instead of finding a home in the `protected/extensions` folder, the documentation states to place it in `protected/modules`, which doesn't exist by default, but can be created (`http://www.yiiframework.com/doc/guide/1.1/en/basics.module`).

Next, a few simple changes must be made to the main configuration file in `protected/config/main.php`. In the `import` section, add a line for `application.modules.srbac.controllers.SBaseController`.

In the modules section, where you'll find the configuration for Gii, add this:

```
'srbac' => array(
  'userclass'=>'User',
  'userid'=>'id',
  'username'=>'username',
  'delimeter'=>'@',
  'debug'=>true,
  'pageSize'=>10,
  'superUser' =>'Authority',
  'css'=>'srbac.css',
  'layout'=>
  'application.views.layouts.main',
  'notAuthorizedView'=> 'srbac.views.authitem.unauthorized',
  'alwaysAllowed'=>array(
    'SiteLogin','SiteLogout','SiteIndex','SiteAdmin',
    'SiteError', 'SiteContact'),
```

```
'userActions'=>array('Show','View','List'),
'listBoxNumberOfLines' => 15,
'imagesPath' => 'srbac.images',
'imagesPack'=>'noia',
'iconText'=>true,
'header'=>'srbac.views.authitem.header',
'footer'=>'srbac.views.authitem.footer',
'showHeader'=>true,
'showFooter'=>true,
'alwaysAllowedPath'=>'srbac.components',
)
```

These are some standard settings as expressed in the SRBAC documentation. A few things to note here are that you must specify exactly what your user class and username fields are. You'll find that at the top of the list. Also, you can set actions that should always be allowed in the `alwaysAllowed` item. This would be useful if you want anonymous users to see your `PostIndex` page. The last major thing to note is the `debug` option. It is very important to set this to `false` as soon as you have properly configured your roles. Most importantly, you will need to assign the Authority role to a user, as this is the only role allowed to administer SRBAC. If you set this to `false` before assigning that role, you will be locked out of further configuration of SRBAC rules. You can reset this to `true` if that is the case.

In the `components` section of your `main.php` config, you must set the `authManager` item to SRBAC:

```
'authManager'=>array(
  'class'=>'application.modules.srbac.components.SDbAuthManager',
  'connectionID'=>'db',
  'itemTable'=>'authitem',
  'assignmentTable'=>'authassignment',
  'itemChildTable'=>'authitemchild',
),
```

SRBAC uses three database tables for rules; roles, tasks, and operations will go into the item table. The item child table deals with relationships between roles and tasks, and tasks and operations. The assignment table relates roles to users. These tables will be created during the install process, which will take place the first time you attempt to access SRBAC.

Once you have the SRBAC module in the `modules` folder and the config options set in `main.php`, you can visit your site `index.php?r=srbac`, and you should be taken to the install screen. This screen will show you a summary of the settings and will have an install button at the bottom. This action will create the tables necessary for using SRBAC in your application.

To set up rules for a particular controller, you must first make a few changes to the controller file. Instead of extending `Controller`, it must now extend `SBaseController`. By relying on a higher level controller, the checking for permission upon action request is abstracted away from you as a coder. It becomes something you don't need to think about, and it doesn't clutter up your code:

```
class PostController extends SBaseController
```

At the top of your controller, under the `public $layout` setting, you'll need to set up a couple of quick variable definitions to avoid issues in your views:

```
public $layout='//layouts/column2';
public $breadcrumbs;
public $menu;
```

Lastly, you can remove the `filters` and `accessRules` methods:

```
/**
 * @return array action filters
 */
public function filters()
{
    return array(
        'accessControl', // perform access control for CRUD operations
        'postOnly + delete', // we only allow deletion via POST
request
    );
}

/**
 * Specifies the access control rules.
 * This method is used by the 'accessControl' filter.
 * @return array access control rules
 */
public function accessRules()
{
    return array(
        array('allow',  // allow all users to perform 'index' and
'view' actions
            'actions'=>array('index','view'),
            'users'=>array('*'),
        ),
        array('allow', // allow authenticated user to perform 'create'
and 'update' actions
            'actions'=>array('create','update'),
```

```
                    'users'=>array('@'),
            ),
            array('allow', // allow admin user to perform 'admin' and
    'delete' actions
                    'actions'=>array('admin','delete', 'pending'),
                    'users'=>array('admin'),
            ),
            array('deny',  // deny all users
                    'users'=>array('*'),
            ),
        );
    }
```

Now you are ready to go back into SRBAC. If you go to the **Managing AuthItems** section, you should see a link for **Autocreate Auth Items**. This page will show you controllers that you are able to use to autogenerate tasks and operations. By clicking on the light bulb icon next to a listed controller, you should see on the right a list of all the operations that it can create as well as two default tasks that it wants to set up for you. You can selectively choose items or go with **Select All**. For tasks, you can go with the two standard tasks of viewing and administering, and either stick with these, add more, or create entirely unique tasks for your controller.

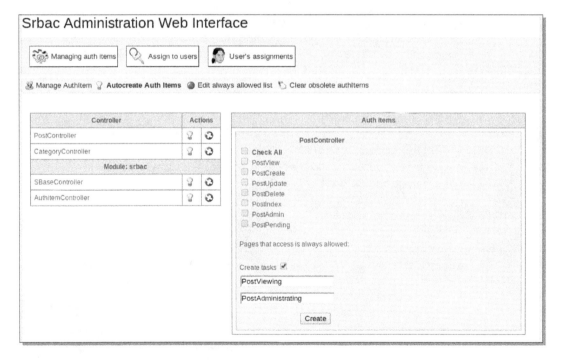

After autogenerating your tasks and operations, you'll want to set up a few roles. Go back to the primary **Auth Items** screen and find the **Create** button. Here is where you can create custom tasks and operations, but you will find this most useful for simply creating roles. Change the drop-down to role, give it a name, and hit **Create** below. Note that you have to hit **Create** on the left side before adding another role.

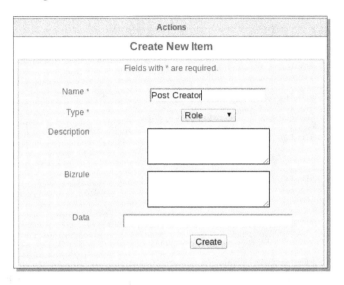

At this point, we can go to the **Assign Roles to Users** section. This is a simple, graphical way to add and remove assignments.

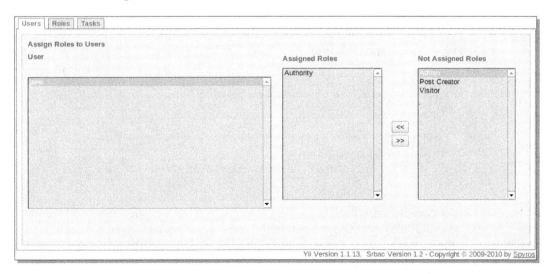

With a few clicks, you can assign operations to tasks, tasks to roles, and roles to users. Make sure you add the Authority role to at least one user, as mentioned earlier, before you turn of SRBAC debug-mode in the `main.php` config file.

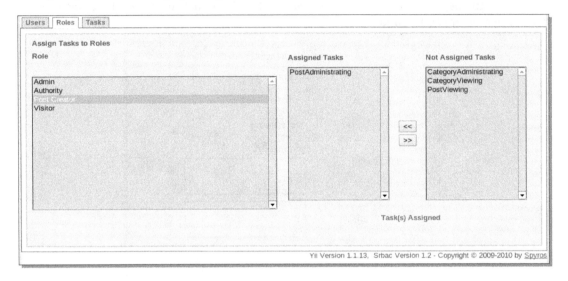

SRBAC is useful in more situations than simply managing controller actions. When we set up the drop-down menu earlier, we restricted the pending menu option to be visible only to the admin user:

```
array(
    'label'=>'Pending',
    'url'=>array('/post/pending'),
    'visible'=>Yii::app()->user->name=='admin'
),
```

Now that we have roles, we can set up this restriction based on roles:

```
array(
    'label'=>'Pending',
    'url'=>array('/post/pending'),
    'visible'=>Yii::app()->user->checkAccess('Admin')
),
```

At any point in our code, we can check to see if the current user has a particular authorization assignment. This could be a role, task, or operation. This is important because it's not enough to simply show the user a denied access message when they visit part of the app they shouldn't be using. It's better that they never find a link to it in the first place.

People and places you should get to know

Finally, let's see where we can find more information about the Yii framework, as well as its community.

Yii website

The framework website is, quite simply, the number one place to read more about Yii. Its URL is `http://www.yiiframework.com`. As with any software tool, the API documentation section will be invaluable as you work through your development. The forums provide an excellent resource for getting help with specific issues you run into. There are a number of tutorials, as well as a wiki with examples to look at. The best outside resources are listed on the website as well, so this should absolutely be your first stop.

API

The Yii API documentation is probably the most beautiful and easy to use documentation ever published on the World Wide Web. The URL is `http://www.yiiframework.com/doc/api/`. If you are going to seriously use Yii, you definitely should add it to your bookmarks, because you'll need it a lot.

Tutorials and guides

+ The Yii website has a number of tutorials that are excellent. One of the best resources beyond the API itself is the *Definitive Guide* found at `http://www.yiiframework.com/doc/guide/`. This guide is very thorough, covers all the important topics, and has a lot of important tips and code samples packed in.

+ The blog demo we based the book on is discussed in great length in the tutorials section of the Yii website. The URL is `http://www.yiiframework.com/doc/blog/`.

+ The wiki holds a lot of independent examples and code snippets that should come in handy (`http://www.yiiframework.com/wiki/`).

+ If you can't find an example of what you're trying to do in the wiki, the forums are also a great resource to search for previously solved solutions to problems. With Yii's popularity on the rise, the forums are increasingly active. This is an excellent place to get your questions answered.

+ One of the most comprehensive tutorials for Yii was done by Larry Ullman. He has written an excellent book on Yii, and has chosen to release much of the content publicly on his website `http://www.larryullman.com/series/learning-the-yii-framework/`.

+ There's another set of excellent screencasts produced by Jeffrey Winesett to help you get started at `http://www.yiiframework.com/screencasts/`

IRC

You can find the Yii community on Freenode in the `#Yii` channel.

Twitter

Follow updates and changes to the framework by following `@YiiFramework`.

Facebook

Yii has even entered the Facebook world with a group for everything Yii-related (`https://www.facebook.com/groups/61355672149/`).

At the time of writing, there were several thousands of members.

Thank you for buying
Instant Yii 1.1 Application Development Starter

About Packt Publishing

Packt, pronounced 'packed', published its first book "*Mastering phpMyAdmin for Effective MySQL Management*" in April 2004 and subsequently continued to specialize in publishing highly focused books on specific technologies and solutions.

Our books and publications share the experiences of your fellow IT professionals in adapting and customizing today's systems, applications, and frameworks. Our solution based books give you the knowledge and power to customize the software and technologies you're using to get the job done. Packt books are more specific and less general than the IT books you have seen in the past. Our unique business model allows us to bring you more focused information, giving you more of what you need to know, and less of what you don't.

Packt is a modern, yet unique publishing company, which focuses on producing quality, cutting-edge books for communities of developers, administrators, and newbies alike. For more information, please visit our website: www.packtpub.com.

Writing for Packt

We welcome all inquiries from people who are interested in authoring. Book proposals should be sent to author@packtpub.com. If your book idea is still at an early stage and you would like to discuss it first before writing a formal book proposal, contact us; one of our commissioning editors will get in touch with you.

We're not just looking for published authors; if you have strong technical skills but no writing experience, our experienced editors can help you develop a writing career, or simply get some additional reward for your expertise.

PUBLISHING

Agile Web Application Development with
Yii1.1 and PHP5

ISBN: 978-1-84719-958-4 Paperback: 368 pages

Fast-track your Web application development by
hamessing the power of the Yii PHP framework

1. A step-by-step guide to creating a modern,
   sophisticated web application using an incremental
   and iterative approach to software development

2. Build a real-world, user-based, database-driven
   project task management application using the Yii
   development framework

3. Take a test-driven design (TDD) approach to
   software development utilizing the Yii testing
   framework

Yii Rapid Application Development
Hotshot

ISBN: 978-1-84951-750-8 Paperback: 340 pages

Become a RAD hotspot with Yii, the world's most popular
PHP framework

1. A series of projects to help you learn Yii and Rapid
   Application Development

2. Learn how to build and incorporate key web
   technologies

3. Use as a cookbook to look up key concepts, or work
   on the projects from start to finish for a complete
   web application

Please check **www.PacktPub.com** for information on our titles

Web Application Development with Yii and PHP

ISBN: 978-1-84951-872-7   Paperback: 332 pages

Learn the Yii application development framework by tacking a step-by-step approach to building a Web-based project task tracking system from conception through production deployment

1. A step-by-step guide to creating a modern Web application using PHP, MySQL, and Yii

2. Build a real-world, user-based, database-driven project task management application using the Yii development framework

3. Start with a general idea, and finish with deploying to production, learning everything about Yii in between, from Active record to Zii component library

Yii 1.1 Application Development Cookbook

ISBN: 978-1-84951-548-1   Paperback: 392 pages

Over 80 recipes to help you master using the Yii PHP framework

1. Learn to use Yii more efficiently through plentiful Yii recipes on diverse topics

2. Make the most efficient use of your controller and views and reuse them

3. Automate error tracking and understand the Yii log and stack trace

Please check **www.PacktPub.com** for information on our titles